GIFTS OF THE SPIRIT FOR KIDS

WRITTEN BY **JESSI GILL**

ILLUSTRATED BY TEETONKA ILLUSTRATIONS

Gifts of the Spirit (for Kids)

Trilogy Christian Publishers, a Wholly Owned Subsidary of the Trinity Broadcasting Network

2442 Michelle Drive, Tustin, CA 92780

Trilogy Christian Publishing/TBN and colophon are trademarks of Trinity Broadcasting Network.

For information about special discounts for bulk purchases, please contact Trilogy Christian Publishing.

Trilogy Disclaimer: The views and content expressed in this book are those of the author and may not necessarily reflect the views and doctrine of Trilogy Christian Publishing or the Trinity Broadcasting Network.

Manufactured in the United States of America

10 9 8 7 6 5 4 3 2 1

Library of Congress Cataloging-in-Publication Data is available.

ISBN: 979-8-89041-300-0

E-ISBN: 979-8-89041-301-7

"Direct your children onto the right path, and when they are older, they will not leave it."

Proverbs 22:6 NLT

Did you know
    you have an amazing gift?

I do too!
We all do.

God
has blessed the body of
Christ with many gifts.

These are called
the gifts of the Spirit.

They are wisdom, knowledge, faith, healing, miracles, prophecy, tongues (speaking and understanding), and discernment of spirits.

You can have more than one gift, and each one is important.

None is lesser than another.

Everyone has different gifts, so we all must work together.

Being a part of the body of Christ requires teamwork.

We need all the people with all the gifts, and we don't take sides.

All these gifts come
from the same Spirit.
That is the Spirit of God.

That is what unites us as one body
of Christ. And a body needs all of its
parts to work right.

So, I ask you,
what is your gift?